SHAPES

Ovals

by Julia Vogel
illustrated by Sharon Holm

Content Consultant: Paula J. Maida, Ph.D.
Department of Mathematics, Western Connecticut State University

magic wagon

visit us at
www.abdopublishing.com

Published by Magic Wagon, a division of the ABDO Publishing Group, 8000 West 78th Street, Edina, Minnesota, 55439. Copyright © 2008 by Abdo Consulting Group, Inc. International copyrights reserved in all countries. All rights reserved. No part of this book may be reproduced in any form without written permission from the publisher. Looking Glass Library™ is a trademark and logo of Magic Wagon.

Printed in the United States.

Text by Julia Vogel
Illustrations by Sharon Holm
Edited by Patricia Stockland
Interior layout and design by Becky Daum
Cover design by Becky Daum

Library of Congress Cataloging-in-Publication Data
Vogel, Julia.
  Ovals / Julia Vogel ; illustrated by Sharon Holm.
      p. cm. — (Shapes)
  ISBN 978-1-60270-045-1
1. Ovals—Juvenile literature. 2. Geometry, Plane—Juvenile literature. 3. Shapes—Juvenile literature. I. Holm, Sharon Lane, ill. II. Title.
QA483.V64 2008
516'.154—dc22
                                        2007004718

Ovals are each place you look.

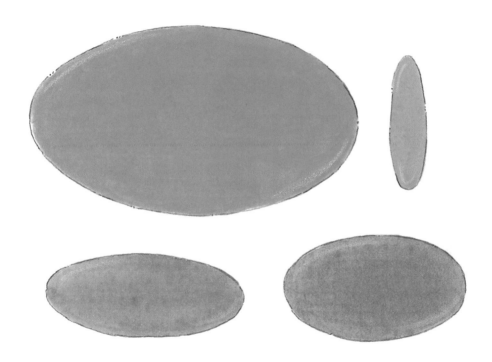

Can you find them in this book?

A curve that gently bends around,

an egg-like oval you have found.

5

Use an oval when you eat.

Take an oval for a treat.

Find an oval in this room.

See an oval that goes "Zoom!"

9

Wear an oval on your head.

Wear an oval colored red.

Turn an oval on the door.

Use an oval on the floor.

Try an oval for a snack.

Wear an oval on your back.

Pick a melon from a vine.

Pick an oval that tastes fine.

Catch an oval in a game.

Catch an oval you can name.

Chase an oval with a friend.

Chase an oval to the end.

Ovals are hiding all around.

How many ovals have you found?

23

I Spy an Oval Game

Look around. Find an oval. Then say: "I spy an oval that is…" and name its color. Everyone has to guess what oval you see. Then it is someone else's turn to spy an oval. You can guess what it is.

Count the Ovals Game

Pick a room in your home. Count how many ovals you can find.

Words to Know

line: a long thin mark.

melon: a large, rounded fruit.

oval: a curved, egg-like shape, like a stretched or squashed circle.

shape: the form or look something has.